HOW DOES IT WORK?: FARM TECH
PLANTERS

by Johannah Luza

pogo

Ideas for Parents and Teachers

Pogo Books let children practice reading informational text while introducing them to nonfiction features such as headings, labels, sidebars, maps, and diagrams, as well as a table of contents, glossary, and index.

Carefully leveled text with a strong photo match offers early fluent readers the support they need to succeed.

Before Reading

- "Walk" through the book and point out the various nonfiction features. Ask the student what purpose each feature serves.
- Look at the glossary together. Read and discuss the words.

Read the Book

- Have the child read the book independently.
- Invite him or her to list questions that arise from reading.

After Reading

- Discuss the child's questions. Talk about how he or she might find answers to those questions.
- Prompt the child to think more. Ask: Can you name some of the ways planter technology has improved?

Pogo Books are published by Jump!
5357 Penn Avenue South
Minneapolis, MN 55419
www.jumplibrary.com

Copyright © 2024 Jump!
International copyright reserved in all countries.
No part of this book may be reproduced in any form without written permission from the publisher.

Library of Congress Cataloging-in-Publication Data

Names: Luza, Johannah, author.
Title: Planters / Johannah Luza.
Description: Minneapolis, MN: Jump!, Inc., [2024]
Series: How Does It Work?: Farm Tech | Includes index.
Audience: Ages 7-10
Identifiers: LCCN 2023012897 (print)
LCCN 2023012898 (ebook)
ISBN 9798885246941 (hardcover)
ISBN 9798885246958 (paperback)
ISBN 9798885246965 (ebook)
Subjects: LCSH: Planters (Agricultural machinery) — Juvenile literature. | Planting (Plant culture) —Juvenile literature. | Instructional and educational works.
Classification: LCC TJ1483 .L89 2024 (print)
LCC TJ1483 (ebook)
DDC 681/.7631—dc23/eng/20230330
LC record available at https://lccn.loc.gov/2023012897
LC ebook record available at https://lccn.loc.gov/2023012898

Editor: Eliza Leahy
Designer: Emma Almgren-Bersie
Content Consultant: Santosh K. Pitla, Ph.D., Biological Systems Engineering

Photo Credits: John Rehg/Shutterstock, cover; oticki/Shutterstock, 1, 15; hudiemm/iStock, 3; Ilike/Shutterstock, 4; Glasshouse Images/Alamy, 5; North Wind Picture Archives/Alamy, 6-7; Dan Van Den Broeke/Dreamstime, 8; Budimir Jevtic/Shutterstock, 9; Sergii_Petruk/Shutterstock, 10-11; JJ Gouin/Alamy, 12-13; Jamesboy Nuchaikong/Shutterstock, 14; chinahbzyg/Shutterstock, 16-17; Design Pics Inc/Alamy, 18-19; Ekaterina Pokrovsky/Shutterstock, 20-21; Vereshchagin Dmitry/Shutterstock, 23.

Printed in the United States of America at Corporate Graphics in North Mankato, Minnesota.

TABLE OF CONTENTS

CHAPTER 1

. . . .

WHAT IS A PLANTER?

Have you ever planted seeds?
Did you plant one seed at a time?

In the early days, farmers planted seeds and **crops** by hand.

In the 1850s, the first planters were invented. Horses pulled them. Farmers walked behind the planters. They raised and lowered handles to drop seeds. This was more **efficient** than planting by hand.

CHAPTER 2

HOW DO PLANTERS WORK?

Today, planters are large machines. Farmers pull them with tractors. Planters plant crops, such as corn and beans, in rows.

tractor

planter

Planters plant seeds at the right depth. They also plant them the right distance from one another. This helps crops grow better. Farmers get a better **yield**.

A planter stores seeds in a seed hopper. Discs and row cleaners with jagged edges clear away debris like twigs and old roots. A furrow opener digs a **trench**.

DID YOU KNOW?

One type of planter is called a seeder or seed drill. These plant smaller seeds, such as grains, close together. Why? Grains don't need as much space to grow as other crops.

seed
hopper

row
cleaner

furrow
opener

disc

back wheels ·····▶

A seed falls through the bottom of the seed hopper. It goes into a seed plate. The gauge wheel turns the seed plate. It releases the seed. The seed is placed a certain distance from the last seed. A seed firmer pushes the seed down. Two back wheels then cover the trench with dirt.

TAKE A LOOK!

What are the parts of a modern planter? Take a look!

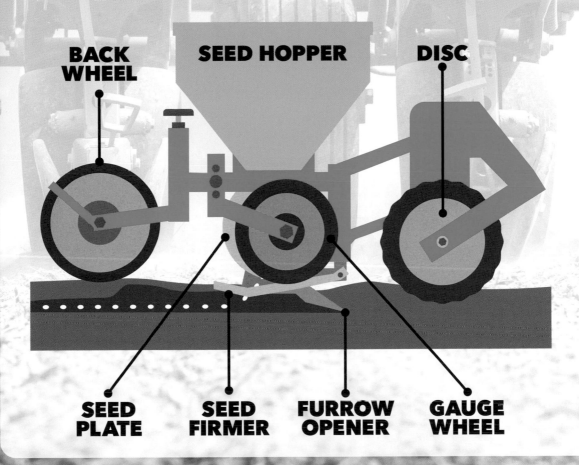

BACK WHEEL

SEED HOPPER

DISC

SEED PLATE

SEED FIRMER

FURROW OPENER

GAUGE WHEEL

CHAPTER 3

NEW TECHNOLOGY

With better technology, planters can help farmers even more. Planters plant more crops with fewer workers. This saves farmers money. One modern planter can plant 720 seeds a second!

cornfield

How else can planters help? Farmers lose crops to **drought** or **floods**. New planter technology boosts crop yields in different soil conditions.

Most modern planters spread **fertilizer** when they plant seeds. Some fertilizers have harsh chemicals. These chemicals can be bad for the **environment**.

DID YOU KNOW?

Fertilizer has **nutrients** that help plants grow. But too much fertilizer can **pollute** water.

fertilizer

liquid fertilizer
tank

Sensors help planters use less fertilizer. The sensors know exactly where seeds are planted. The planter sprays fertilizer only on the seeds. This lessens the amount of pollution.

New technology leads to better crop yield, less pollution, and less work. How else do you think new planter technology can help?

ACTIVITIES & TOOLS

PLANTER MATH

Machines help us do tasks more efficiently. See how planters help us do more in this math activity!

What You Need:
- paper
- a pencil or pen
- calculator

Do the following math problems:

1. Two hundred years ago, a farmer could plant just 1 acre of corn a day. Now, some planters can plant 500 acres of corn a day. Can you write an equation to find out how many acres of corn a farmer can plant in 30 days?

2. Some modern planters can plant 720 seeds in one second. How many seeds could these planters plant in 60 seconds?

GLOSSARY

crops: Plants grown for food or profit.

drought: A long period without rain.

efficient: Working very well and not wasting time or energy.

environment: The natural surroundings of living things, such as the air, land, or sea.

fertilizer: A substance you can put in the soil to make it richer so that plants grow better.

floods: Great amounts of water that rise and spread over the land.

nutrients: Substances such as proteins, minerals, or vitamins that plants and animals need to stay healthy.

pollute: To contaminate or make dirty, especially with products made by humans.

robots: Machines that are programmed to perform complex human tasks and that sometimes resemble human beings.

sensors: Tools that can detect and measure changes and send the information to controlling devices.

trench: A long, narrow ditch.

yield: The amount or quantity of something produced.

INDEX

TO LEARN MORE

Finding more information is as easy as 1, 2, 3.

1. Go to www.factsurfer.com
2. Enter "planters" into the search box.
3. Choose your book to see a list of websites.

FACT SURFER